Nuneaton
Past & Present

John Burton

John Burton

Dec' 2000

SUTTON PUBLISHING LIMITED

Sutton Publishing Limited
Phoenix Mill · Thrupp · Stroud
Gloucestershire · GL5 2BU

First published 2000

Title page photograph: Nuneaton from the chimney of the Electric Light Station, run by Nuneaton Corporation, during the first decade of the twentieth century. The large building with its chimney in the right foreground is the flour mill. In the immediate foreground is Mill Walk. Beyond that can be seen Bridge Street, and on the upper left is the old Newdegate Arms Hotel, and the bank, now HSBC; to its right is Parsons, Sherwin, with their showrooms and early garage.

British Library Cataloguing in Publication Data
A catalogue record for this book is available from the British Library.

ISBN 0-7509-2712-7

Typeset in 10.5/13.5 Photina.
Typesetting and origination by
Sutton Publishing Limited.
Printed and bound in England by
J.H. Haynes & Co. Ltd, Sparkford.

For Ted Veasey,
who started it all

CONTENTS

Nuneaton Town Centre, decorated and ready for celebration, on Charter Day in 1907. The first mayor of the town was Joseph Fielding Johnson, a successful businessman and entrepreneur.

INTRODUCTION

To be asked to produce a book which mirrors the sort of slide show I have been presenting in the area for many years was too good an opportunity to be missed. It is a source of constant fascination to most residents of any town to be able to see past and present photographs of a particular spot. So much the better if one or other of the photographs shows a present home, workplace or area with special memories or associations.

A volume such as this is not the sort of history book to which one refers for hard facts, and by its nature it can only cover a small area of even a small town. Readers will note that there are areas of the town and aspects of its industry and life which are not covered. Thus, Chilvers Coton is the only suburb or outlying parish to be covered. This is not because Attleborough, Stockingford, Weddington, Chapel End or Hartshill, for instance, are unimportant. It seemed sensible to show a reasonable cross section of the town and its most important neighbouring parish, rather than to cover every area and industry superficially. The hope is that if this volume is successful there will be a second one which can deal with other suburbs and the now only remembered industries like mining, ribbon weaving and the extractive industries, which formed such a vital part of Nuneaton's history.

Inevitably some of the pictures will be familiar from other publications: there is only a limited number of views of the Market Place or Bridge Street; but what is new about this volume is the linking of the old views with pictures taken, whenever possible, from the same spot some twenty, fifty or hundred years later. Younger readers particularly will find the contrasts interesting. Older readers will enjoy the nostalgic journey through time. Both will enjoy, I hope, the fact that the ninety modern pictures have all been taken in the millennial year, and will themselves form a series of pictures which will inform future generations about the appearance of the town in the year 2000.

There are very few buildings in Nuneaton over a hundred years old. As the town became more prosperous in the 1890s the reaction then, as now, was to use new-found wealth to rebuild, and most of the attractive buildings date from the period 1890–1910. Much has been lost, but less than in some other towns, and there is pleasure to be gained from careful observation of buildings, especially above the ground floor.

Nuneaton and Bedworth Borough Council rightly takes pride in its floral displays. Indeed the borough has achieved commendable success throughout the 1990s. Only when one sets out to photograph a town comprehensively does one become aware of blind spots which are often unremarked. I have been in turn amazed and annoyed by the proliferation of street furniture which constantly detracts from the visual appearance of the town. There is, though this is not confined to Nuneaton, a forest of metal posts with direction signs, prohibition signs and warning signs, many of which are unnecessary, and most of which are placed without any regard for the visual impact they have on the aesthetic appearance of the town. Almost without exception the metal posts that support this information overkill are not perpendicular. All this seems a pity when you consider how attractive the flowers and the new pedestrian areas are in the town, and the efforts which have been made throughout the borough to portray significant symbols of our past through public art, which enhances the appearance and interest of the town.

1

Town Centre

A view from the Electric Light Company's chimney, which stood behind the present town hall, before 1910. In the foreground is Coventry Street, with the Congregational church on the left. On the right is the town clock and Market Place. Along the top of the picture is Abbey Street. The factory recently revealed between Queen's Road and Stratford Street can be seen in the middle of the picture. The building is now hidden again behind the new development at the Queen's Road end of the Market Place. The church steeple visible in the top centre of the picture was the Wesley Methodist chapel at the corner of Stratford Street and Abbey Street.

Nuneaton Market Place in late Victorian times. It is part of the fascination of Nuneaton that a weekly market has been held on this site for seven hundred years. This picture was taken from an upper room in the Crystal Palace (see page 17) and shows the town before the 1890s rebuilding. Thus the town clock is not there, neither is the bank (now Barclays). The Peacock has not yet been rebuilt. (*Susan Womersley collection*)

The picture below was taken in the 1930s and by then the buildings we know now were in place, although almost every one has new owners or tenants. These were days when you could prop your bike against the kerb, do your shopping, and find the bike still there on your return.

The Market Place, late 1940s. The Board Inn has acquired some half-hearted timbering, or a painted version of it. Tudor Nuneaton as it never was! There is even less traffic in this picture than in modern pedestrianised days.

   The picture below had three delivery vehicles when I went to photograph it in September 2000. Patience was rewarded when they eventually drove away.

The Board Inn, Market Place. This delightful picture is actually half of a postcard dated about 1909 – a tribute to the photographic quality of early pictures. The Star Tea Company delivery vehicle was outside their shop, which had transferred from the other side of the Market Place in 1905.

Not quite from the same spot as the picture opposite. It needed a contortionist's skill for the photographer to avoid the scaffolding on the building to the left, and the multiplicity of 'For Sale' signs on the building under the clock, empty for several years. However, to its credit, this day in August 2000 was one of the few during the year when the water feature was working.

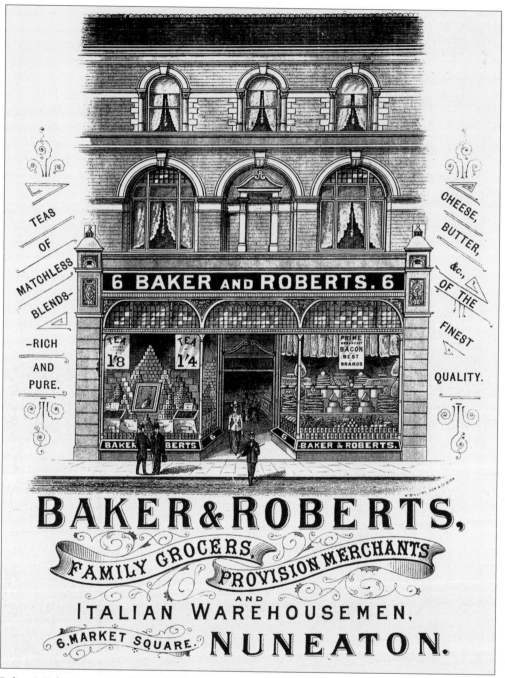

Baker & Roberts was a splendid shop in a fascinating building. There were several other buildings with decorated windows in the town. Older residents have spoken of the delightful aroma of coffee beans wafting across the Market Place. This advertisement comes from a short history/guide to the town produced in 1900.

Marks and Spencer has replaced the block which housed Baker & Roberts, and now appears to be retreating behind the greening of Nuneaton. Placing trees in town centres needs great care, especially in narrow streets. It is interesting to note how the Midland & Counties Bank, now Barclays, with its delightful late 1890s terracotta, uses a similar window design to the Baker & Roberts building.

THE LARGEST AND MOST COMPLETE STOCK OF

General Drapery, Millinery, Mantles, &c., in the District.

Dressmaking by Experienced Assistants.

9 & 10, THE MARKET PLACE, NUNEATON.

Castle's drapery store in the Market Place, 1900. The advertisement appears to have undergone some darkroom manipulation of the flag.

The building occupied by Castles was later taken over by Woolworths, and this lovely picture shows the staff sitting outside the store sometime in the late 1940s. At one time Woolworths prided themselves on selling nothing more expensive than 6d.

The picture below shows the same building in August 2000. Our Price was originally Boots, with its distinctive house design. This one dates from 1907 and replaced the Star Tea Company.

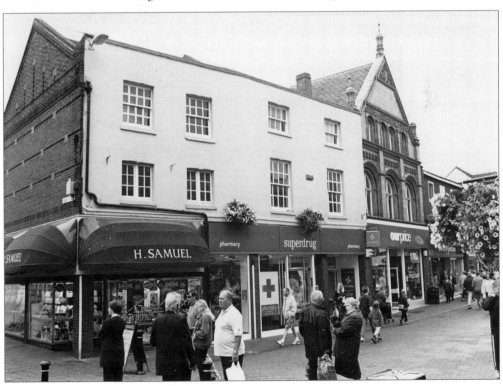

South side of Market Place, late nineteenth century, showing the much older White Hart next to Brown's Commercial Hotel. The picture on page 6 shows this line in relation to the rest of the Market Place.

   The replacement buildings below were built in the 1970s and 1980s and show more of a variety than would have been the case had they been built ten years earlier. The picture was taken in August 2000.

The picture above was painted by the talented local artist Patty Townsend, and it was one of several produced for a book about George Eliot Country published in 1890. This one was called Milby Market Place, after *Scenes from Clerical Life*. Patty Townsend was the second wife of Joseph Fielding Johnson (1840–1917), first mayor of Nuneaton in 1907. They lived at Attleborough Hall. Patty died of cancer in 1907. (*Nuneaton Museum and Art Gallery*)

    The picture below was taken in September 2000. The stall on the right is for guide dogs, and the one in the distance is for Local Agenda 21, encouraging sustainability. One of the ubiquitous market researchers, complete with clipboard, is sitting on the left.

Market Place, looking west. The picture above is from a 1906 postcard; the one below was taken in September 2000. Charles Clay has been replaced by Boots. The Bradford & Bingley was originally Smiths Bazaar, but was replaced by a lovely building in 1908. The carved stone over the entrance is worth studying in this well-proportioned town centre building. I'm not sure about the trees.

Queens Road end of the Market Place, *c*. 1908. The Crystal Palace was a popular public house and variety hall which was pulled down in 1909 to widen the entrance into Queens Road. The narrow entrance indicates the early gate-wide way into the market which controlled entry for traders. (*Peter Lee collection*)

The picture below (September 2000) shows the distinctive new building which was completed in 1999.

A straightforward past and present pair separated by about sixty years. They show the Market Place viewed from Queens Road. In the top picture the banner hanging from the shop is outside Boots. The picture below shows a busy Friday in September 2000.

Very similar views to those on the opposite page, but the picture above shows the impact the River Anker has had on the town. With depressing regularity heavy rain caused the river to burst its banks and flood homes, shops and offices throughout the town. It was not until the flood relief scheme across Weddington some thirty years ago that the town centre became safe from disastrous flooding. The picture above was taken in 1932.

Remarkably similar pictures separated by fifty years. The buildings on the left, variously the library, council offices and fire station have disappeared, but the ordinary artisan dwellings on the right have survived against all the odds.

These two pictures show the same section of Queens Road as the ones opposite, but from the other direction. The picture below shows the old council offices again, but the picture above takes us back probably to the 1880s and shows the earlier Red Lion in the distance. The Wash brook flows under the bridge in the middle of the photograph.

ROYAL :: Perfect Pictures
ROYAL ELECTRIC HALL, STRATFORD STREET, NUNEATON.

The LATEST LIVING PICTURES & HIGH-CLASS VARIETY.

7 TWICE NIGHTLY **9**

Sole Proprietor :
E. A. SHUTE.

Manager :
J H. PHILLIPS.

:: TELEPHONE 5y1. ::

A detour into Stratford Street takes us to the site of the old Royal Electric Hall, shown here in an advertisement from 1910. A chapel before becoming a cinema, the building was later taken over by a printer before it was redeveloped in the 1980s.

The redeveloped site shows a sensitive piece of planning which retains an echo of the former building in the gable of the new. Colemans moved from their former shop in Queens Road.

The essentially residential nature of Queens Road can be seen in the picture above, where most premises on the left are still private homes. Dugdale Street is on the right. The picture above was taken before the war, and before the splendid art deco Co-op building seen below in the August 2000 view.

Same policeman, different photographers!
The picture on the right is looking to the
right of Dugdale Street; the one below
shows the town centre side of the Dugdale
Street corner. These both show the 1932
floods, and by then many families possessed
box brownie cameras and recorded the
event. The smaller picture was loaned to the
author by Alan Garner from Doncaster, who
lived in Nuneaton until 1950. The picture
below was from an unknown local. The
pictures beg the question that if the town
was flooded as far as Dugdale Street, exactly
what traffic was there for the policeman to
direct from the safety of his beer crate?

The picture above was taken in the 1920s before the Co-op Hall was built. In a sad state of repair, it never recovered from a disastrous fire in the 1960s and Kwik Save does little to enhance its appearance. Behind it all is a splendid 1930s building which deserves a new life. The chapel on the corner of Edward Street disappeared in the 1960s to be replaced by a nondescript group of shops. The long roof with skylights was the photographic studio of Chettle, and then Openshaw.

Largely unaltered at a superficial glance, but in fact the bottom of the street was lost to the new inner ring road. Many of the roads in this part of Nuneaton follow a regular planned pattern and were designed for the expanding workforce coming to live in the town during the first decade of the twentieth century.

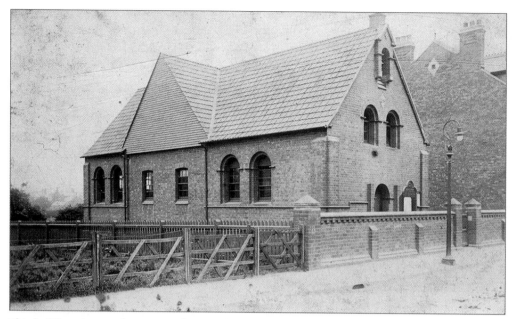

This building shows a fascinating change of use which reflects the changing population make-up of the area. It was built in 1899 as a mission church to serve the expanding area of terraced housing off Queens Road, built without a pub because of the patrician influence of Reginald Stanley, a staunch Methodist teetotaller.

The picture below shows the same building, altered and expanded, in August 2000, but now serving as a day centre for the largely Muslim community living in the area.

The influence of the twelfth-century priory has already been seen in the Market Place, which drew the town from the other side of the river where it had nestled as a Saxon village. The priory was able to make money from the market rights, and from Abbey Street. In the early twentieth century the dreadful courts and hovels in Abbey Street which had provided a high proportion of Nuneaton's homes were eased by development of new edge-of-town estates off Queens Road, and Abbey Street became the main shopping area, helped by the presence of the once mighty Co-op.

The shop on the left of the picture above was owned by F.R. Jones, a printer and bookseller, who deserves adulation for the huge number of local postcards he produced between 1900 and 1910. He often worked with a local photographer from Stockingford, Bradbury, and their combined output has done much to illuminate our knowledge of what the town looked like before the First World War.

The Gate Temperance Hotel was built by Reginald Stanley in 1898. It is best described as exuberant and is one of those buildings that even people with no interest in architecture notice. If it were built as a film set it would cause amusement, but it is a much-loved building, despite the fact that it replaced a half-timbered house.

Reginald Stanley's touching faith in the Temperance Movement was not shared by enough of the Nuneaton miners and workers to make it a profitable venture, and it closed after a few years. The ground floor is now occupied by a building society. One wonders whether they would have given a mortgage for the original.

The north side of Abbey Street, a few yards from the Alliance & Leicester. Part of the building shown in the 1920s view on the left is still there. Baker has been replaced by Gilesports in the August 2000 view.

Abbey Street in the 1950s is still recognisable today. The Liberal Club was another Reginald Stanley building which remains, though with a new use. The Methodist church on the corner of Stratford Street has gone. The tree-lined street obscures the buildings and is better photographed in winter, although the hanging baskets are not as successful as their summer counterparts.

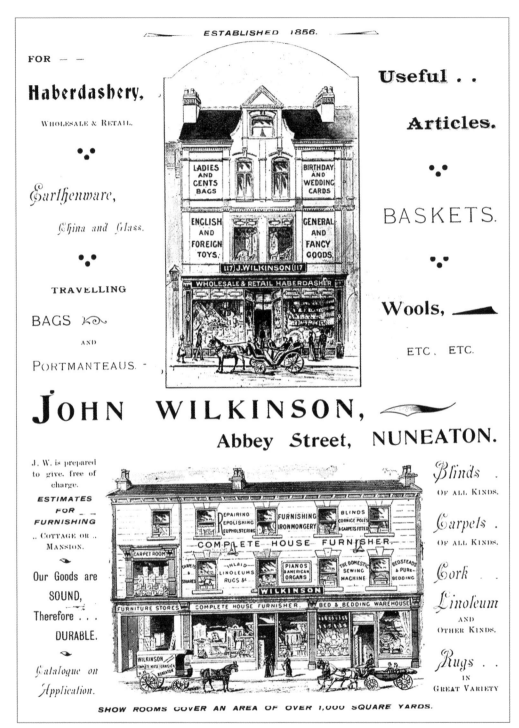

Wilkinson's advertisement from 1900. This was a well-established business with shops on both sides of Abbey Street. The bottom engraving shows the building on the south (Co-op) side of the street, which was demolished and rebuilt in a very unusual and interesting design in 1903. The building was eventually taken over by the Co-op.

The distinctive design at roof level, seen in the engraving opposite, can still be seen in Abbey Street, as this August 2000 picture shows. Wilkinson's was the shop on the left. On the brickwork at first-floor level can still be seen traces of advertisements for men's suits at 37s 6d and similar prices.

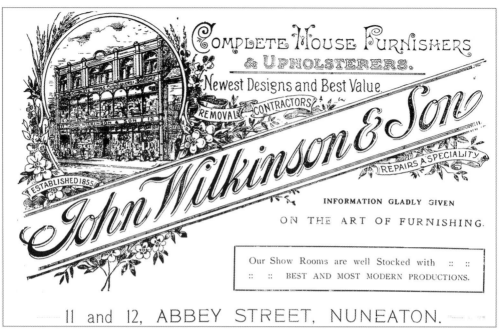

This advertisement for Wilkinson's shows the shop after the rebuilding in 1903. The illustration was in a 1911 publication. The picture below, taken in August 2000, shows the same building with its distinctive windows. The whole frontage of the Co-op was repainted and smartened in 2000 and reflects great credit on those responsible. It has given a sensitive treatment to an interesting line of buildings.

NUNEATON CO-OPERATIVE SOCIETY, LTD.

Central Stores: 13 to 19, ABBEY STREET.

Branch No. 1,
HIGH STREET,
BEDWORTH.

Branch No. 2,
NEW BUILDINGS,
ANSLEY.

Branch No. 3,
ATTLEBOROUGH.

Branch No. 4,
WHITTLEFORD.

Branch No. 5,
STOCKINGFORD.

Branch No. 6,
EDWARD STREET

A Branch Store will
shortly be opened at
BULKINGTON,
to serve Ryton,
Ansty,
Shilton,
Wolvey,
and surrounding
districts.

WORKING MEN are INVITED to JOIN the above Society and to PURCHASE their GOODS from the Shop where they will *Share the Profits.*

IT IS MAINLY upon CO-OPERATION that you must rely for the Improvement of your Social Position.

The advertisement dates from 1911, and the earnest seriousness of the Co-operative movement is reflected in the text. They really did share the profits then, but why didn't the Co-op shout it from the rooftops when Tesco and Sainsbury produced their pale imitation reward cards? Above ground-floor level there is a labyrinth of corridors and meeting rooms which the public knows nothing of.

The Bull's Head can be seen on the extreme right of the 1908 picture below. The advertisement dates from 1910, and shows an interesting, if somewhat esoteric, selection of groups who used Joe Smith's pub as their headquarters. One wonders exactly what the Sheffield Equalised Order of Druids did – and how often.

Abbey Street, Nuneaton.

The Bull's Head is dead; long live The Courtyard. The pub was completely refurbished and now offers food and entertainment that Joe Smith could not have dreamed of in 1910. The building remains and it has been a sympathetic conversion, as the August 2000 picture shows.

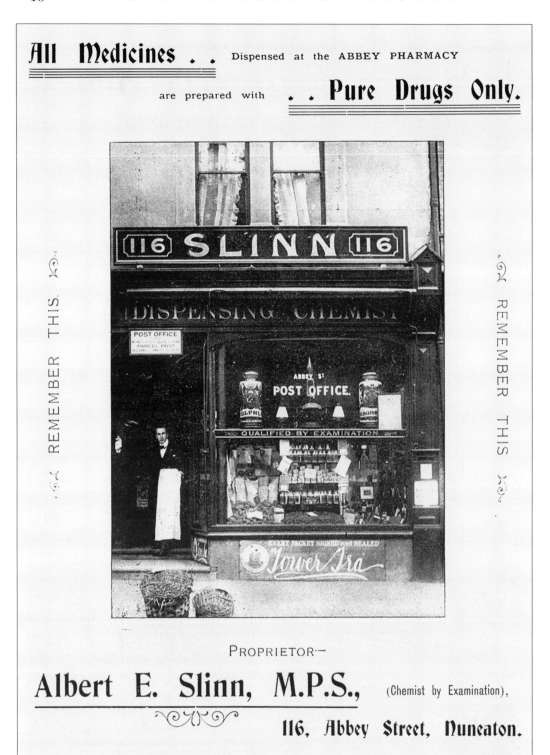

All Medicines . .   Dispensed at the ABBEY PHARMACY

are prepared with   **. . Pure Drugs Only.**

REMEMBER THIS.

REMEMBER THIS

PROPRIETOR:—

Albert E. Slinn, M.P.S.,   (Chemist by Examination),

116, Abbey Street, Nuneaton.

No. 116 Abbey Street was a sub-post office as well as Slinn's chemist and pharmacy when this advertisement was produced in 1900. Presumably Mr Slinn himself is the man in the doorway.

By 1910 Mr Slinn had departed and the shop was taken over by Henry Lester, who also had a branch in Bridge Street. The picture below shows the sign outside the shop, next door to Wilkinson's at 117 Abbey Street. This postcard was produced in the 1920s. An interesting item in the advertisement above is the provision of a darkroom for the use of Nuneaton's enthusiastic amateur photographers.

Nearly eighty years separate these pictures yet only the property to the left of the Scala has been rebuilt. It is very unusual for original buildings like these in a town centre to have withstood the onslaughts of the last century. The Scala is quite a handsome building, dating from 1914, and it saw service as one of several cinemas in the town.

The new inner ring road cut Abbey Street in half. Originally it, or Upper Abbey Street, contained a mixture of housing and small shops but 1960s and 1970s redevelopment has turned most of the street into houses and flats, and the road is choked with cars of people wishing to avoid parking fees. The Coach and Horses has not survived a change of name and now, in August 2000, stands empty.

The picture above was taken by the author in 1980. Strip away the shop windows and the advertising boards and there was a fine gentleman's town house on the corner of the street. The site was required for the inner ring road and the picture below (August 2000) shows the full extent of the planning gain. The Leisure Music building is the Elliott Sales building above.

The Plough and Ball before 1900 shown on a postcard produced in about 1904 by Bradbury, who actually sent the card to a friend, pointing out that he had used some of his own older collection for his new cards. The Town Talk replaced it soon afterwards and has recently (2000) been superbly restored outside – a credit to those responsible.

The angle in the picture below is further to the right for a really accurate comparison, but the difference is to make a point. The top picture shows Abbey Green as a small community with children in the street some time around 1920. (*Ted Veasey collection*)

The picture below shows Abbey Green on a good day since the traffic is moving. The community has been cut in half by the advent of the motor car, which clogs up this junction at most times of the day.

Bottrill Street is typical of the edge of town expansion to serve the workers in the growing industries in Nuneaton. The picture above shows a boiler being delivered to Hall and Phillips' hat factory before the war. The Prince of Wales, later Edward VIII, visited the factory in July 1934, but as the picture below (August 2000) shows the hat factory has gone and modern housing is being built.

There are several splendid photographs of butchers in Nuneaton. It is not clear which one this is but it might be at Abbey Green. The butcher, proudly displaying his meat in a way which would give modern food inspectors apoplectic fits, has also managed to obscure the name above his shop.

The Parker family have been butchers in Nuneaton for over a hundred years. The picture shows their house at Abbey Green before it was converted to a shop in 1905. In the door is Mrs Eliza Brown with the infant Frank in her arms. The children in front are Eliza, Mabel and Lizzie.

The house on the corner was converted into a shop in 1905. Shown here are Mary 'Polly' Leadbetter with Mabel and Tom Brown.

Frank Parker continues the family business and after a century it seemed appropriate to line up the staff in time-honoured way, minus the carcases and three staff who were on holiday in August 2000. From left to right they are Martin Fenn, Phillip Batch, Anne Simpson, Maureen Jordan, Joan Parker, Carl Hutchinson, Frank Parker, Ian Johnson, Joe Brown and Jon Parker.

The print above dates from 1729 and shows the ruins of the once thriving priory, established to the west of Eatun in the 1150s. The effect was to draw the village across the Anker, establish a market, and hence market traders, and stretch the newly forming town west along the length of what we now call Abbey Street. This pattern survived the dissolution of the monasteries by Henry VIII. Expansion of the town in the late nineteenth century necessitated a new parish and the priory ruins were gradually altered from 1876 onwards, and St Mary's Abbey Church was the result, shown below in about 1910.

The rebuilt Abbey Church incorporates part of the original nave and crossing. The priory site was extensive and is still revealing its secrets. It deserves to be better known. The picture above shows the newly restored church in 1905, and the picture below shows part of the new housing in Bottrill Street in August 2000.

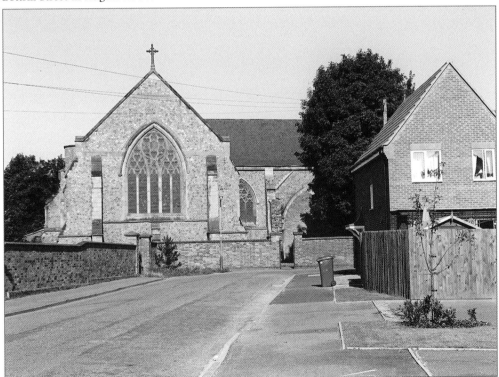

Little apparent change here over a ninety year period. Manor Court Road in 1910 was a recently established and highly desirable new road of substantial houses, for businessmen who had risen in the world and wanted a house which reflected their status. Reginald Stanley built his mansion opposite the abbey, and the new road linked with the Cock and Bear and the canal at the top of what we now call Queens Road.

The Corporation Street/Newtown Road roundabout is one of the biggest in the town. The picture above shows the flower beds on the island looking east in 1998. During 2000 a transformation produced this stunning fountain, inspired by our twin town of Roanne. The picture below shows car number one competing in the Millennium Rally on August Bank Holiday Sunday, 2000.

Another view of the floods in 1932. This is looking down Newtown Road. The town's tendency to flood was presumably not lost on the group constructing the carnival float shown below. There must have been times when residents felt a direct line to Noah would be a distinct advantage. (*Alan Garner collection*)

Part of the oldest area of Nuneaton, and a continuation of the old village street along the east side of the river. From this end of the street the villagers would have gone out to work the open fields towards Watling Street. The coming of the railways totally altered the topography of the area. The picture above shows the newer Crown Inn with much older farmhouses beside it about a hundred years ago. (*Ted Veasey collection*)

The August 2000 picture shows a rebuilt pub without the oldest buildings, but with the same line of nineteenth-century dwellings following the ancient village pattern.

The first Trent Valley station was built when the railway opened in 1847. The picture above from the 1920s shows the third station and the picture below, taken in August 2000, shows the much enhanced approach to the station in a scheme funded jointly by the borough council and Central Rail during 1999.

From a 1900 publication, the picture above shows the line of cottages in Bond Gate that came down to make way for the theatre which, when it actually opened, was called the Prince of Wales, and later the Hippodrome. The building on the left of the picture is still there.

The picture below shows an early view of the interior of the theatre. (*Ted Veasey collection*)

The Prince of Wales Theatre soon after it opened in 1900. The theatre served Nuneaton for some sixty years before it closed in the face of the television age. The large model of Euterpe, the Greek muse of lyric poetry, was rescued from the roof and now resides in some glory in the local history gallery of the museum.

The building that eventually replaced the theatre, which remained derelict and partially demolished for about twenty years. This photograph was taken in August 2000.

The postcard above was produced before 1910 and shows the old Hollybush on the corner. The picture below shows the modern building which is no longer a pub. Traffic over the Leicester Road bridge was clearly less of a problem in 1910 than it is now.

Bond Gate was always the first to suffer when the Anker burst its banks, but along with Church Street it is the original Saxon village settlement. Bond Gate at present is a mess and seems only to be a funnel for traffic.

The postcard above dates from 1907 and shows Bond Gate when it functioned as part of the town that people lived in and traded in. The Conservative Club is one of Nuneaton's finest buildings, though it has lost many of the ornate art nouveau decorations. It deserves a better fate and could make wonderful offices or flats.

This is part of the town which has seen a lot of redevelopment, some of it good but much of it indifferent. The picture above dates from about 1900. Only one building remains on the picture below, taken in August 2000, and that is the Pen and Wig pub, formerly the Queens Head, identified by the two gable ends.

Domesday Book records the presence of a water mill in 1086. The mill shown here was built in 1886 and lasted until the 1960s.

The flour mill was demolished and replaced by this building, which is used by the DSS. It would be good to see a major attempt to bring the Anker back into life as part of the town landscape. At present it is attractive only in Riversley Park.

The picture above is a watercolour by Patty Townsend showing Church Street, or Orchard Street, in George Eliot's *Janet's Repentance*. The street included the house of Lawyer Dempster (Buchanan in reality), and the Pettifers. The houses had long gardens down to the river, now the George Eliot Memorial Gardens. This line of houses was destroyed by bombs in 1941, and after the war plans were drawn up for the redevelopment of the area, to include a civic centre. What happened? This forgotten part of Nuneaton was actually where the village started, and nearly sixty years after it was bombed we still have wooden huts in the centre of the town.

The 1905 postcard view of Church Street above shows the mixture of private residences and owner-occupied shops which made up the street. All the buildings on the right have gone, to make way for largely indifferent 1960s replacements. The only exception is Frederick Gibberd's library, designed to be part of the redeveloped civic area after the war, and a superb building, the first in a series of excellent library buildings which now include Leamington and Rugby. A pity therefore that when the county authorities had to install disabled access they made do with cheap yellow brick instead of the stone which Gibberd's building deserves. A pity too that the cool grace of the foyer is spoiled by the obtrusive backs of bookcases for leaflets.

EVERY . .

ACCOMMODATION

. . FOR

Cyclists, . . .

Footballers, .

And all Athletes .

And Visitors. . .

PRESENT.   *Photo. by Miss Blakeman.*

QUEEN'S HEAD HOTEL.

Church · Street, · Nuneaton.

Proprietor: **G. H. TAYLOR.**

COMFORTABLE SMOKE ROOM.

HARMONY EVERY MONDAY, FRIDAY, & SATURDAY.

Headquarters of the Nuneaton Fanciers' . . . Society. . . .

 WELL AIRED BEDS.

PAST.

CHOPS AND STEAKS.

A delightful advertisement from 1900 showing the Queen's Head past and present, the theme of this book and proving the point that there is nothing new! Mr Taylor was no doubt delighted with his new pub. He must have been quite a character to achieve Harmony on a Friday or Saturday night in Nuneaton.

Now renamed the Pen and Wig, the pub still looks good, especially after its recent refurbishment. Like the similar Town Talk at Abbey Green (see page 45), this is a strong confident building.

The Bull Hotel, a fine coaching house in Bridge Street. The entrance to the courtyard was moved to the right at some time in the last century. The pub features as the Red Lion in George Eliot's *Janet's Repentance*.

ARCH. CARMICHAEL, QUEEN'S ROAD.
MY HAIRDRESSER.
ESTABLISHED A WEEK BEFORE THE FLOOD.

The British ability to turn adversity on its head is shown beautifully in this postcard from the enterprising Mr Carmichael, who lived in times when religion was sufficiently observed for his readers to have heard of Noah and to be able to make the connection with a wry smile. The flood referred to was in late December, 1900.

The August 2000 photograph below shows the much refurbished pub and restaurant with its newer name, the George Eliot Hotel.

The picture above shows Bridge Street in the 1890s; the building on the right was the Nuneaton Brewery. It may have been converted from a disused flour store belonging to John Knowles who owned the mill. It was not unusual for millers, used to grinding malt, to take an interest in brewing. Starting in 1878, it never seems to have succeeded. By 1907, when the postcard below was produced, the site had been sold and redeveloped.

The pictures on these two pages show four stages of development in Bridge Street. The picture above shows the redeveloped left-hand side of the street. The entry to the flour mill which used to be at the side of W.H. Smith disappeared with the old buildings.

The picture below from August 2000 shows the pedestrianised street, though there seem to be as many vehicles as in the picture above when traffic was allowed. The canopy flowers over Debenhams are a delight every year. It is a shame they aren't on the left-hand side as well.

Another brewery picture. The site extended back as far as Newdegate Street and the Conservative Club was built on part of the brewery land. John Knowles sold the business in 1881, and it changed hands again the following year. Water analysis suggested that the quality matched that at Burton-on-Trent, but new brewers Adams Holford only lasted for about six years. The picture below shows the Bridge Street and Church Street corner following the severe floods on 30–31 December 1900.

The same view in August 2000. Debenham's building is pleasant and unpretentious.

A lovely view of shops packed with goods – the sort of street you want to walk down – from a postcard sold in about 1920 by W.H. Smith, who happen to feature in the picture. The view below was taken in August 2000.

When the Newdegate Arms Hotel was demolished in the 1960s (see overleaf) it was replaced by Heron Way shopping precinct, seen above. (*Dennis collection*) By the 1990s it was showing signs of fatigue and was reborn as Abbeygate (shown below), a covered shopping area which links Abbey Street with Harefield Road.

The "NEWDEGATE ARMS" :: NUNEATON.

FAMILY & COMMERCIAL HOTEL and POSTING HOUSE.

Recommended by the R.A.C., A.A., and M.U.

Posting in all its Branches.

Stabling for 80 Horses, and Loose Boxes for Hunters.

Excellent Accommodation for Gentlemen Hunters.

Billiards.   Electric Light.

Good Accommodation for Motorists,

Wedding Carriages, Broughams, &c.

'Bus meets all Trains.

Telephone No. 84.   ::   Proprietor : T. J. LILLEY.

A Depot for Motor Repairs, Petrol, Tyres, and Accessories, is within 50 yards of the Hotel, at the **Nuneaton Garage (Parsons, Sherwin & Co., Ltd.),** Official Repairers to the R.A.C., M.U. and C.   **Cars for Hire.   Telephone 84.**

The advertisement for the Newdegate Arms appeared in 1910 at a time when horses were still important, hence the mention of stabling for eighty horses. Where would you put eighty horses today? But they realised that cars were the coming thing by pointing out the proximity of the Nuneaton Garage. Linked to this building had been the manor court, an important part of early administration for the town. It was known then as the Crown Inn, and later The Bull. The picture below places it in a context which is still recognisable.

The Newdegate Arms shown opposite was demolished in 1914 to ease traffic problems. The replacement building was excellent but did not survive the 1960s. Had it managed to last another fifteen years it would have prospered with conference facilities and proximity to the NEC. After the war Kathleen Ferrier and Roy Henderson came to sing in Bedworth and the Newdegate Arms refused to accommodate 'show people'! The George Eliot statue, visible in the picture below, stands near the entrance to the hotel. One wonders what she would have said about such provincialism.

HINCKLEY ESTABLISHMENT.

Telegrams :
Parsons,
Nuneaton,
Hinckley, and
Coventry.

Telephone :
No. 24,
Nuneaton.
Coventry,
No. 312.

NUNEATON ESTABLISHMENT.

C. Parsons,

GENERAL AND
FURNISHING • IRONMONGER,

Nuneaton, Hinckley, and Coventry.

METAL TRADES' VALUER   BUSINESS TRANSFER AGENT

The Stock at the several depots consists of a complete assortment of Furnishing and Builders' Ironmongery. Bar Iron, Steel, Oils, Colours, Paints, Agricultural Implements.

In the working departments between 20 and 30 hands are employed in the manufacture of Iron Fencing. Palisading, Gates, Gas Fittings, Electric and Crank Bell Hangings ; Manufacturing, Fixing, and Repairing Agricultural Implements and Machinery. . . . .

The new premises will, when finished, rank among the finest in the Kingdom for the display of Iron-mongery, Grates, Mantels, Gas Fittings, Etc. . . .

The building will con-tain a floor space of over 10,000 square feet in ad-dition to the present ware-houses. . . . . . .

NEW PREMISES IN COURSE OF ERECTION,

COVENTRY ESTABLISHMENT.

NEW BRIDGE STREET, NUNEATON.

Parsons were well established in Nuneaton by 1900 when this advertisement appeared. Indeed they were expanding, as the fine frontage of their new store shows. New Bridge Street is now Newdegate Street.

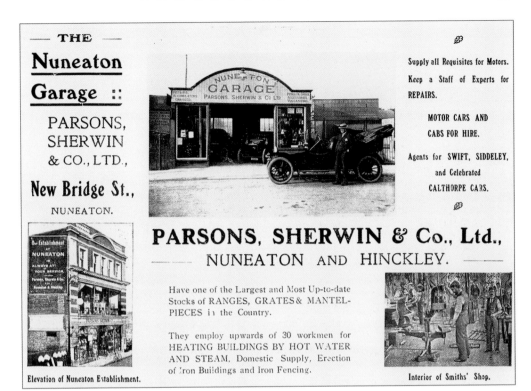

THE Nuneaton Garage ::

PARSONS, SHERWIN & CO., LTD.,

New Bridge St.,
NUNEATON.

Supply all Requisites for Motors.

Keep a Staff of Experts for REPAIRS.

MOTOR CARS AND CABS FOR HIRE.

Agents for SWIFT, SIDDELEY, and Celebrated CALTHORPE CARS.

Elevation of Nuneaton Establishment.

PARSONS, SHERWIN & Co., Ltd.,
NUNEATON AND HINCKLEY.

Have one of the Largest and Most Up-to-date Stocks of RANGES, GRATES & MANTEL-PIECES in the Country.

They employ upwards of 30 workmen for HEATING BUILDINGS BY HOT WATER AND STEAM, Domestic Supply, Erection of Iron Buildings and Iron Fencing.

Interior of Smiths' Shop.

By 1911, when this advertisement appeared, Parsons had joined with Sherwin and they had expanded into the new motor car service industry. They had a branch in Hinckley, and during the 1920s they took over Linney and Horrobin in Bedworth.

The picture below shows the site in August 2000, with the building in use as a club and bar, having earlier been a store and then head office for Triton showers.

Harefield Road was the edge of town, largely occupied by the cattle market. The very grainy newspaper reproduction above dates from April 1925 and shows the premises of Mr W. Croshaw's Nuneaton Motor Company. It adjoined the cattle market and was the town's Authorised Ford Depot. it looks as if it has strayed from a Western film.

Opposite the site of the garage in Harefield Road is now the bus station with its 1990s shelters and interesting 1950s clock tower.

The superb picture above dates from about 1890 and shows the old town hall in the distance, where the town clock is now. The building on the corner of Mill Walk stands where Hawkins is in the picture below. The river was later diverted and the Wash Brook, seen in the foreground, was culverted to where it is now visible joining the Anker by the DSS building. The houses behind the telegraph pole were demolished to widen Coventry Street. The picture below was taken during the Millennium Rally on August Bank Holiday, 2000.

This section of Coton Road is blessed with several good buildings. The law courts are on the left of
the picture above, though now occupied by Yorkshire Bank. The town hall was built in 1934 to a
Georgian design by Peacock and Bewlay of Birmingham. Many of the original fittings remain and
the building looks more distinguished with the passage of time. Having castigated the library for its
disabled access, it has to be said that the provision for the town hall is exemplary and might have
been part of the original design.

Above is the free library, built in 1899, and a confident expression through its architecture of the importance of learning, reading and self-improvement. The building only lasted thirty-five years as the site was purchased to enable the town hall to be built to the left of it. The shop visible on the left was the photographic studio of Mr Clare Speight, a man of considerable skill from a family of photographers based in Rugby. The picture below shows the council house. A new building so close to a good older one is a challenge to any architect. Is the solution to copy, to complement or to challenge? The exterior of this works well. Inside, the stairwells are cramped and claustrophobic.

The picture above shows the new town hall under construction when the Anker flooded in 1932. The ground-floor window frames are visible and there must have been several hundred thousand gallons of Anker in the cellars. The chimney and building behind it was the Electric Light Company, and on the extreme right of the picture is the library. On the left is George Eliot Building, a pleasingly proportioned 1926 corner block. (*Josephine Rose collection*)

The picture below shows floods in 1958. The Midland Red bus depot was built near the site of the old library.

The picture above shows the old Congregational chapel which dated from 1793. It has every appearance of a non-conformist church, whereas the replacement (below) which was built in 1903 is a much more flamboyant building. The United Reformed church now shares a minister with the Old Meeting church in Bedworth.

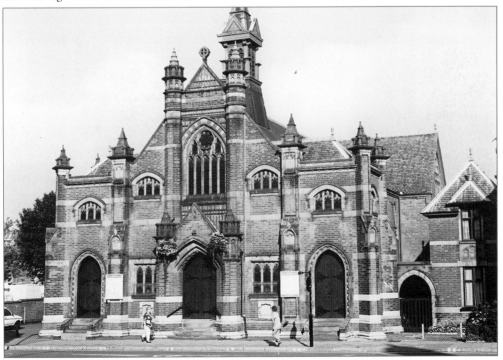

These two are not geographically linked but the chronology demands their linking. The picture below shows the unveiling of the memorial to the men who died in the Boer War. It was originally in Bond Gate (see page 62) by the river, and the town was packed with soldiers and spectators for the visit of General Buller on 28 January 1905. Eventually the figure was moved to the memorial gardens behind the museum, and now it stands near to Coton Road but opposite the Ex-Servicemen's Club, an entirely appropriate location, as the picture to the left shows.

The postcard above dates from about 1922, after the war memorial was in place. Riversley Park had opened in 1907 and ten years later the art gallery was presented to the town, as the park had been, by Alderman Melly. In 1990 the art gallery, which during the 1960s had also become a museum, was enlarged. It has a valuable collection of George Eliot artefacts and a varied programme of exhibitions. The picture below (August 2000) shows the lovely floral displays. The one above looks drab and it is not enhanced by the pieces of artillery either side of the building, purchased to help pay off the First World War debt.

Coton Road (above) before the dual carriageway, *c.* 1920. The building on the left was opened as a cookery and handicraft centre at a time when schools could not afford such specialist rooms and teachers to go with them. This one, built in 1913, is a fine building which has been ruined outside by the addition of a 1960s corridor down the Riversley Road side. It is too depressing to show such insensitivity so the picture below is taken from a different angle!

The picture above shows what a pleasant, wide, comfortably residential road it was. Those on the left had back gardens looking over Riversley Park, but very little of the original remains. Much went to make way for the dual carriageway, and further up the road the older terraced housing has been replaced by blocks of flats.

The picture above shows an exciting day for Coton Road residents early in the last century. A performing bear had come to town, and he can be seen behind the cart. Performing bears are not politically correct these days, but round the corner in Avenue Road the Cedar Tree uses Brewster the bear to entertain children. In this picture are Gemma Morris, Chloe Beasley, Brewster himself with help from Gemma Arnold, Lauri Neale and Brandon Jeffcoat, all enjoying August Bank Holiday, 2000.

2

Chilvers Coton

Part of the kissing gate, which is among the undergrowth alongside the entrance to the graveyard of Chilvers Coton parish church.

The kissing gate on page 93 is shown in this 1905 postcard when Coventry Road provided a better entrance to the churchyard than it does now. The church appears to be quite rural. It was largely destroyed by enemy action in 1941 but was rebuilt by German prisoners of war. The picture below shows the church as it is now.

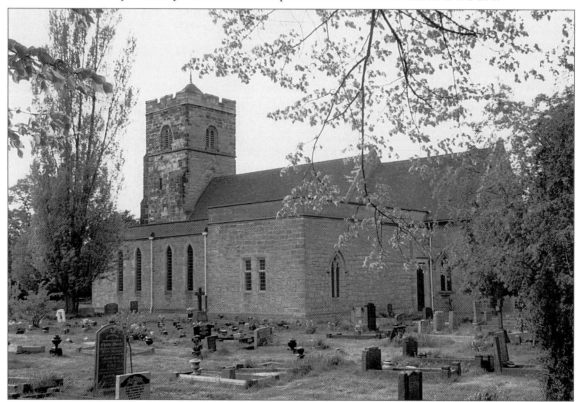

The lovely photograph above shows how rural parts of Chilvers Coton used to be. This is now Avenue Road carrying a heavy traffic load between Coton and Attleborough, and out towards the A5. In 1905 it was a tranquil spot where the Wem Brook was bridged or forded. This view is looking towards Coton Arches and a horse drinks from the stream while the children pose for the camera.

Below we see Graham Coupland with some friends who happened to be around on August Bank Holiday Sunday, 2000, with his horse and trap, and who agreed to pose for the author in the same spot as that seen in 1905.

Coton House was a substantial building on the town side of the Coventry Canal. Local residents remember it in use by the sea cadets. This postcard dates from 1929. When the building was demolished Shepperton Court, an old people's complex, was erected on the site. It is seen here in August 2000.

The Old Wharf Inn, shown above in the 1920s, was a canalside pub with a long history, and for some time it was a listed building. Some years ago it was removed from English Heritage's 'list', and within weeks was demolished. The houses (photographed below in August 2000) on the main road and Watersbridge Gardens are on the site.

F.R. Jones has already been mentioned on page 29. The picture above, taken in 1905, was produced and sold by him. His importance to local historians is that only a local photographer with local interests would bother to produce a card such as this, which might only sell in small numbers. He or she, and there were some female photographers, went into the side roads or attended local celebrations, to the benefit of all of us a century later. The lovely line of trees shown in the winter was replaced by inter-war housing, pictured below in August 2000.

College Street, Chilvers Coton, in 1929 (above) and 2000 (below). An example of little change over seventy years, except for double glazing, central heating and cars. For some reason this part of Chilvers Coton was known as Virgin's End. Out of respect for Chilvers Coton the apostrophe comes before rather than after the 's'.

The Jolly Colliers Inn was a popular pub in College Street and it is shown in this pre-war picture. The pub was pulled down when the A444 by-pass was constructed. (*Mallabone collection*)

The roundabout below is the junction of the by-pass and College Street. From the footbridge over the road you can see the whole of Nuneaton, Hinckley in the distance, and the escarpment near Bradgate Park on a clear day. It was a perfect spot to place the last piece of granite to be taken from the Tuttle Hill quarry, where it overlooks the town that has earned much of its living from the extractive industries. Unfortunately, having placed the rock there, the local authority has not placed any information nearby to tell the curious, or the visitor, what it is and why it is there.

The College for the Poor was a Victorian euphemism for the workhouse, a word which struck terror into the hearts of any likely to go there. This was built in 1800 and was a hugely solid building, in use until after the war. The building below is on the same site and is one of the units belonging to the George Eliot NHS Trust.

Bermuda village takes its name from a Newdegate family administrative connection. A less tropical vision would be hard to imagine, but the Bermuda area has undergone a remarkable transformation in the last fifteen years. The whole area was riddled with early pit workings, many only a few feet deep, since the Warwickshire coalfield outcropped here. The poor quality land was opencast and the picture above shows the early stages in 1988. Below is the scene taken from almost the same spot in August 2000. Dairy Crest and RS Components are huge, and in the foreground is the last stage of the entertainment area in course of construction. It includes a cinema complex, restaurants (well, places to eat), fitness and bowling facilities.

The picture above shows the depth of the opencast mining. It really is a large truck at the bottom. This was photographed in 1990, and the picture below of RS Components is, as near as I can estimate, taken from the same spot in August 2000.

Griff Hollows (George Eliot's 'Red Deeps') was once a delightful place for relaxation and walking. The water was an arm of the Coventry Canal which serviced mines on the Arbury estate. Eventually it became redundant and was filled in, so that only a stream remains. The picture below flatters. The stream is clogged with dead cars and shopping trolleys. The spot where Maggie Tulliver had clandestine meetings with Philip Wakem, the son of her father's enemy, is now a haunt of the disaffected. It was landscaped once but such areas need managing, and that, of course, costs money.

3

George Eliot

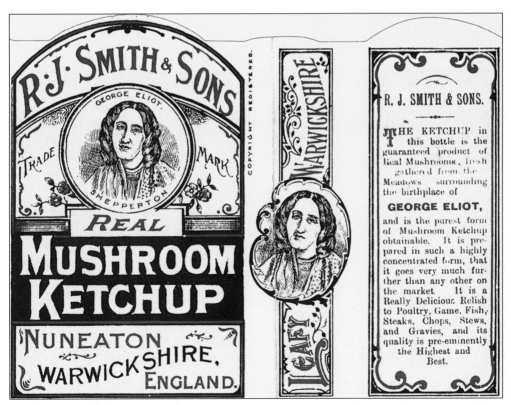

This delightful sauce bottle label was produced in 1906 in R.J. Smith & Sons' factory in Chilvers Coton. Hitching products to famous people is not new, but in this case the famous person had been dead for twenty-six years and her great niece was thoroughly disapproving of seeing the famous relative on a sauce label!

The George Eliot obelisk was originally in Arbury Park, but in 1951 when the George Eliot Memorial Gardens were being laid out, the Newdegate family allowed it to be transferred to its present spot. The picture (left) shows it being put in place.

For the millennium the George Eliot Fellowship, in association with the borough council, redesigned the space in front of the obelisk and had the initials and dates inscribed in the paving. It was completed in time for the wreath-laying ceremony in June 2000.

"George Eliot" Machines are NOT Built like Watches or Guns,

 BUT LIKE = **Cycles.** =

The Details are too smart for jerry-built frame assemblers . . . . to imitate. . . . .

The Success of 1899 Season is our **HIGH=GEARED MACHINES** with **Long Cranks, our own Free Wheel and back=pedal arrange=ments.**

BIRCH'S, NUNEATON.

Another example of the famous author being linked with an unlikely product, even if it was the success of the 1899 season. George Eliot enjoyed her ill health and headaches. A gentle walk would have been the limit of her exercise, and bicycles were still regarded as being for 'fast' women.

The George Eliot Fellowship raised several thousand pounds for their second millennium project, which was to lay paving, flowerbeds and trees round the statue of George Eliot outside the eponymous hospital. The opening was in July 2000. Among the guests pictured above between Bill and Kathleen Adams, chairman and secretary of the Fellowship, are Serena Evans, the guest of honour, with her father Tenniel Evans, and his cousins Robert Winser and Susan Womersley, all descendants of Isaac Evans, Eliot's brother.

There was a lot of interest in George Eliot's origins in Nuneaton and postcards were sold in large quantities with frequent references to the writer. These are two examples and show The Elms, a boarding school run by Mrs Wallington, and a picture of the classroom reputedly used by Mary Anne. This postcard was one of a splendid set produced by photographer Clare Speight in about 1905.

The Elms was pulled down to widen what is now Vicarage Street. The magistrates' courts shown here are built on part of the site and the aerial view below places the school in context with the parish church and the grammar school. The Elms stands nearly opposite the vicarage, on the other side of the road in the top right corner of the picture.

Griff House lies midway between Nuneaton and Bedworth. In George Eliot's day it was part of the Arbury estate. Her family moved to Griff from South Farm when Mary Anne was a few months old, in 1820. It remained home until she was twenty-one, when Robert Evans, her father, retired as land agent to Arbury and moved, with Mary Anne as his housekeeper, to Bird Grove in Coventry, leaving his son Isaac to run Griff. The front of the house has not altered, as the picture below shows.

4

School, Work & Play

FOL-THE-ROL-LOL.

Mac Duff met a girl at Nuneaton,
Her figure had plenty of meat on!
  She said : ' marry me, Mac,
  And you'll find that my back
Is a nice place to warm your cold feet on ! '

83 *(By permission of Fred Leigh, Fred Murray, George
Lashwood, and Francis, Day & Hunter.)*

At the time when these cards were produced, in Edwardian England, people were more reticent where vulgarity was concerned. What happened in private was their own concern. Cards such as this were considered quite bold, and might sometimes be sent in an envelope!

The first school at Abbey Green was built in 1847, one of four Church of England schools. The picture above was a postcard produced in about 1905. Like many schools, it has gone through many transformations but is now a C of E infant school. The picture below was taken in 1907 during the celebrations in the town for the granting of a charter of incorporation, which gave the town a mayor and council. The Abbey Street School float was called 'A Peep in Fairyland'.

'A Peep in Fairyland.' (Abbey Street School).

This was the last day at Abbey for Daniel Smith and Sam Elton. The two six-year-olds were transferring in September 2000 to Weddington, and they were sitting in the old desk (like the one used by the girls in the photograph opposite) with a group of ink wells because the class had been studying what school used to be like.

The picture below was originally going to be of one class, but headteacher Mrs Harrold said that all of Year Two were so lovely that it would be invidious to select one group. So here is all Year Two on the last day of the summer term in 2000 with teachers Yvonne Osborne and Carol Clarke.

The expansion of education, especially secondary education in the early twentieth century, led to the opening of several new schools, including Manor Park in 1928. The picture above shows the original block soon after it opened. Later it became a grammar school, a comprehensive and finally a community comprehensive school.

The picture below shows a class in 1939. The teacher on the left was Miss Record from Bulkington. She recalls discussing with her friend and fellow teacher Edna Richards what they should make of their lives as war broke out. Time takes its toll. Edna died in 2000 and May is living out her twilight years in Norfolk. In 1941, after the bombing of Coventry and Nuneaton, May's pupils wrote some poems. In 1991 some pupils also wrote about war. Some of May's pupils visited the school and poems were exchanged – a fascinating experience for all concerned. (*Alan Farnell collection*)

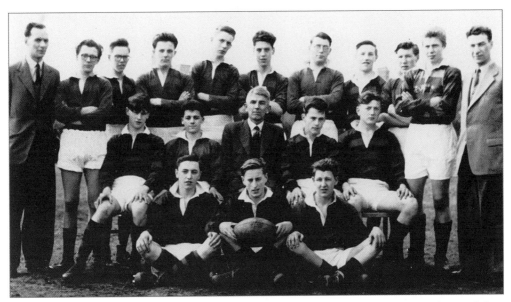

Manor Park Ist Fifteen 1955/6. The school had an enviable sports reputation. Back row, left to right: Mr D. Brinkworth, B. Clarke, T. Briggs, G. Owen, R. Fulford, D. Talbot, K. James. C. Duncan, D. Chapman, R. Haley, Mr G. Kirkbride. Second row: P. Spooner, K. Whitehall, Mr L.J. Goodburn, G. Hudson, R. Jubey. Front row: G. Toon, L. Blackburn, G. Ball. (*Alan Farnell collection*)

The last day of being in Year Eight for this class, studying history on the last day of the summer term, 2000.

King Edward's College, shown above in 1908 and below in 2000. The original school was on the site of the present parish church office, and was rebuilt several times before it moved to the building shown here in 1879. It has an interesting if at times chequered history. It became a sixth-form college, theoretically linked with the North Warwickshire College, in 1973.

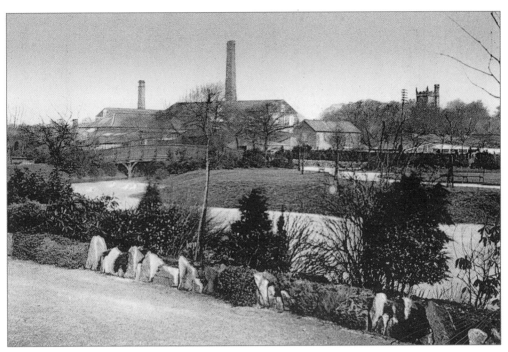

The picture above shows Riversley Park in its early days, but the postcard is chosen because in the distance is the Nuneaton Wool & Leather Works. Tanning had long been an industry in Nuneaton: the river could supply water. When the factory closed Sainsbury's bought the site, as can be seen in the picture below, taken in August 2000.

Some ten years ago when the Stanley brick site was abandoned, there was a huge, secure strongroom housing the firm's records. Eventually vandals succeeded where polite requests had failed to get into the room, and all the records, ledgers, documents and artefacts were soaked with water. Fortunately there was temporary space at the Chilvers Coton Heritage Centre, and the trustees and members of the Nuneaton Society rescued the collection and dried it out, before passing it all on to the County Record Office for evaluation and conservation. The pictures show some of the items saved, and (below) a mould for some of the finials produced by Stanleys.

Established Upwards of a Century.

Stanley Bros., Ltd.,

Brick, Tile, Pipe, Terra-Cotta, and Glazed Brick Works,

NUNEATON.

BRANCH WORKS : BURSLEM (STAFFS.) AND WILLENHALL (NEAR COVENTRY).
COLLIERIES : NUNEATON AND BEDWORTH.

Telegrams :
Stanley's, Nuneaton.

Telephone, No. 12.

ARCHITECTS'
DESIGNS
CARRIED
OUT.

SAMPLES
FREE.

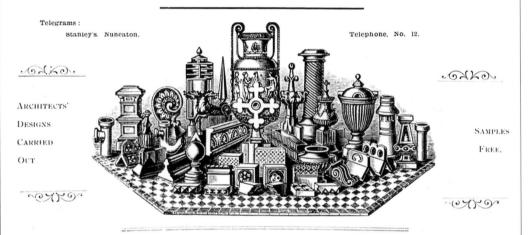

Specialities :

"Improved" Salt-Glazed Bricks,
Brown and Drab Glazed Bricks.
Semi-Encaustic Paving Tiles,
White and Colored Enamelled Bricks.

Blue Bricks. Garden Tiles.	Red Ridges and Finials.	Red and Buff Chimney Pots.	Red, Blue, and Buff Paving Quarries.

BROWN AND CANE-GLAZED SINKS; BLUE KERBING; COPING, &c.

Glazed Socket Pipes and Connections.	Red, Brown, and Blue Roofing Tiles.	Ornamental Vases and Pedestals.

COMPLETE ILLUSTRATED CATALOGUE, CONTAINING MORE THAN 1,000 DESIGNS, ON APPLICATION.

QUOTATIONS GIVEN FOR HOUSE AND STEAM COALS TO ANY STATION.

This advertisement gives some idea of the enormous quantity of high-quality brick and terracotta produced by Stanley Brothers. It comes from a 1900 publication.

Stanley's brickworks in Croft Road: a photograph taken towards the end of production. The picture shows a car parking space in front of the shops in Croft Road, at the bottom of the photograph. The picture below, showing Marsdale Drive, was taken from the same parking space in August 2000.

The Courtaulds factory in Marlborough Road employed hundreds of people at its height. It was a distinctive building, designed to a pattern recognisable in any contemporary Courtaulds. Yet it was built during a period of recession, in 1920. The flat roof was a perennial problem, but the sound of its chiming clock was a distinctive feature of Nuneaton life for those living nearby. The factory stood empty for several years, missed the boom in warehouse conversions and was pulled down, leaving only the symbolic remnant shown below, which is now surrounded by scores of flats. (*Top picture: Weekly Tribune collection*)

The picture above shows the interior of Nuneaton Electric Light Company in 1903. Standing at the switchboard is Mr G.P. Cosway. He was an electrical engineer of some skill, devising methods of insulation which made lighting safer in mines and underground culverts. He became manager of the company, part of which is still owned by the electricity board, as seen below, behind the council house in Coton Road. (*Top picture from Frentzel-Fraser collection*)

Eventually G.P. Cosway opened an electrical engineering firm of his own in Anker Street. The factory buildings are still there, occupied by a company manufacturing heat transfer units. The picture above was taken in the factory, *c.* 1930. (*Frentzel-Fraser collection*) The picture below was taken in August 2000.

Sterling Metals was on the edge of Attleborough, towards Whitestone. It employed hundreds of workers, and was particularly important during the war. Eventually, following retrenchment during the 1970s, the firm closed on its present site and relocated to a smaller unit in Exhall.

The picture below, taken in March 2000, shows how the huge site is being transformed by housing, and was taken from the railway bridge shown in the aeriel view above (*Weekly Tribune collection*)

Before the war, and before television, communities entertained themselves more readily and more often than now. Carnivals, fairs, Whit Walks, all played their part in the annual round and have practically all lost their significance. The picture above shows a charabanc setting off at a Hospital Carnival in the 1930s. (*Malcolm Curtis collection*)

The picture below shows the mayor of Nuneaton & Bedworth for 2000–1, Councillor Diana Hawkes JP, shaking hands with Peter Young, competitor and guiding force behind the Millennium Rally in Nuneaton over August Bank Holiday, 2000.

THE BANDSTAND, RIVERSLEY PARK, NUNEATON

Riversley Park is close to the town centre and to houses, and its riverside and floral displays are a pleasure for all. During the summer the local authority sponsors a series of Sunday concerts in the bandstand. The picture above shows a similar event in about 1920, and the one below shows a group of people relaxing in the August sun with a bottle of wine and music from the band in 2000.